P9-DVH-352

a gift for:

_____

from:

_____

Great at Any Age
Who Did What From Age 1 to 100 . . . and Beyond

Copyright © 2009 by Gift Books From Hallmark, a division of Hallmark Cards, Inc.
Visit us on the Web at www.Hallmark.com.

Compiled and written by Scott Degelman & Associates, Colorado Springs, CO.
Text copyright Scott Degelman & Associates.

Editorial Director: Todd Hafer
Art Director: Kevin Swanson
Design: Myra Colbert Design
Production Artist: Dan Horton

ISBN: 978-1-59530-115-4
BOK2086

Printed and bound in China

GREAT
AT ANY AGE

✳

who did what from
age 1 to 100…and beyond

Hallmark
GIFT BOOKS

GREAT
AT ANY AGE

*

who did what from
age 1 to 100…and beyond

INTRODUCTION

"Age is just a number," notes former Major League pitching great Steve Carlton. And those words aren't just a cliché to the four-time Cy Young Award-winner. He takes them so seriously that he quit keeping track of his birthdays long ago in an effort to free himself from the limitations and expectations that various ages can impose on their "victims."

We admire Carlton's spirit, but with due respect, we think he's looking at things the wrong way. (And, by the way, he's 64, whether he knows it or not.) We believe that the best way to free ourselves from the shackles of age is to celebrate the people who prove that you're never too young, too old, or even too middle-aged to accomplish something significant.

With that goal in mind, we bring you this book, honoring women, men, and children who have refused to let their birthdates build a wall between them and their dreams. You'll read about intriguing feats and milestones in music, science, business, sports, TV and film, medicine, art, technology, and literature. Some of the names you'll encounter will be familiar to you, but you are likely to discover a few new heroes along the way.

Several people pop up multiple times. Their inclusion is very much intentional. In some cases, you'll see how early dedication leads to enduring success. Jack Nicklaus shot 51 for 9 holes at age 10, broke 70 (for 18 holes) at age 13, grabbed the first of his two U.S. Amateur titles at 19, and won his stunning final Masters victory at 46.

Others get multiple mentions for their ability to come back from injury, disappointment, or just plain inactivity. That's why you'll read about swimmer Dara Torres setting a world record at age 15—then returning to win three Olympic silver medals—and set an American record—26 years later. That's why you'll read about 93-year-old Lillian Gish starring in *The Whales of August*—a full 76 years after starring in *The Birth of a Nation*.

So read on. Be intrigued. Be surprised. Be inspired. You're never too old or too young to do something great. (And, as George Foreman, who—at age 45—knocked out Michael Moorer to become the world heavyweight boxing champion will tell you, you're never too middle-aged either.)

*

AGE 0-1

At just 7 days old, Mary, from the House of Stuart, becomes Queen of Scotland.

At 9 months old, future gymnastics star Shawn Johnson displays her prowess by "dismounting" out of her crib.

Eleven-month-old actress/model Brooke Shields lands her first gig—as the Ivory Snow baby.

Eighteen-month-old Mickey Rooney appears in his family's vaudeville act.

AGE 2

Judy Garland begins her stage career.

Hsüan-t'ung becomes Emperor of China.

AGE 3

PuYi becomes Emperor of China. (The Republican Revolution will force him to abdicate his post at age 6.)

A golfing prodigy named Tiger Woods shoots 48 for 9 holes on his hometown golf course in Cypress, California.

Late-bloomer Albert Einstein utters his first words.

Ivan the Terrible becomes Grand Prince of Moscow.

Ernest Hemingway goes fishing for the first time.

AGE 4

Kim Ung-Yong displays fluency in Korean, English, German, and Japanese. (His I.Q. is estimated at 200.)

Upon the death of his father, Louis XIII, young Louis XIV becomes King of France.

Natasha Richardson appears in the film *The Charge of the Light Brigade*, which stars her mother, Vanessa Redgrave.

"I stopped believing in Santa Claus when I was six. Mother took me to see him in a department store and he asked for my autograph."

– SHIRLEY TEMPLE

Prodigy Andre Agassi impresses tennis great Jimmy Connors as the two rally for 15 minutes.

AGE 5

Mountain climber Debora Wilson scales a 4,000-foot peak.

Sir Temulji Nariman marries the newly dubbed Lady Nariman (who is also 5). Despite the arranged marriage, the couple stays wed for 88 years, until Sir Temulji's death.

Charlie Chaplin performs with his mother on the vaudeville stage.

AGE 6

Wolfgang Amadeus Mozart performs piano concerts across Europe.

Actress Shirley Temple receives an honorary Oscar for her contribution to film.

Ron Howard begins his run as Opie Taylor on the TV classic *The Andy Griffith Show*.

Pepi II becomes Pharaoh of Egypt; his reign will span 94 years.

Chinese table tennis player Guo Yue begins her competitive career. (Fourteen years later, she'll be the reigning world champion.)

AGE 7

Though blind and deaf, Helen Keller masters a vocabulary of 625 words.

Future country music star Jerry Reed receives a $7 used guitar and starts honing his skills. He begins experimenting, striking the strings with a thumb pick, which will become one of his trademark techniques.

Michael Tan begins studying for a bachelor's degree in mathematics at New Zealand's Canterbury University.

Olympian-to-be Michael Phelps exhibits excess energy and restlessness due to his ADHD. His mother, in an effort to deal with the problem, enters him in a swimming program.

Stephen King writes his first short story.

Violin virtuoso Yehudi Menuhin solos with the San Francisco Symphony Orchestra.

AGE 8

Actor Justin Henry earns an Oscar nomination (for Best Supporting Actor) for his role in the Dustin Hoffman/Meryl Streep film *Kramer vs. Kramer*.

Mozart composes his first symphony.

Table tennis prodigy Joy Foster wins the Jamaican singles and mixed doubles titles, making her the youngest ever national sports champion.

Future comedian Bernie Mac performs his first stand-up routine—at a church event. His spot-on impersonation of his grandparents earns him a spanking.

Singer and actress Julie Andrews masters a four-octave vocal range.

AGE 9

Genghis Khan assumes the role of chief of his Mongol tribe.

Danica Patrick receives a go-kart as a gift from her father and begins racing around a makeshift oval—marked by paint cans—in the parking lot of her dad's glass store.

Jackie Cooper secures an Academy Award nomination for his role in *Skippy*.

Kirsen Wilhelm bicycles across America. The journey takes her 66 days to complete.

Eighteenth-century mathematician and philosopher Maria Agnesi delivers an hour-long lecture, in Latin, on a woman's right to vote.

Little League baseball pitcher Jericho Scott is ruled ineligible to throw for his New Haven, Connecticut, team. The reason? He throws too hard for a 9-year-old—40 miles an hour. (Scott's team refuses to move him to another position and is therefore disbanded by league officials.)

Boris Karloff, future horror-flick star, plays the role of the demon king in a children's production of *Cinderella*.

Daisy Ashford writes the novel *The Young Visiters*, which will go on to sell more than half a million copies.

AGE 10

Abigail Breslin (*Little Miss Sunshine*) is nominated for the Best Supporting Actress Oscar.

Napoleon enrolls in military school.

Tatum O'Neal wins the Academy Award for Best Supporting Actress for her performance in *Paper Moon*, costarring her father, Ryan O'Neal.

Anne Lewis wins the Women's Professional Rodeo Association barrel racing championship.

Indian actor Kishan, a veteran of 24 films, makes his directorial debut with *C/o Footpath*, which he also writes and stars in.

Jack Nicklaus shoots 51 for 9 holes.

Mary Badham is nominated for Best Supporting Actress for her role as Scout in *To Kill a Mockingbird*.

AGE 11

British figure skater Cecilia Colledge becomes the youngest Winter Olympian ever when she competes at the 1932 Games in Lake Placid, New York, finishing eighth. (Colledge will go on to win a world championship five years later and be credited with inventing the camel and layback spins and the single-foot axel jump.)

Jasmine Plummer quarterbacks her Harvey, Illinois, football team to the Pop Warner Super Bowl, becoming the first female quarterback to achieve that feat. Her story inspires the movie *The Longshots*, featuring Ice Cube and Keke Palmer, star of *Akeelah and the Bee*.

Michael Jackson fronts the Jackson Five as they record their smash hit "ABC."

Brandon De Wilde earns a Best Supporting Actor nomination for his role in the classic western *Shane*.

Figure skating icon Sonja Henie represents Norway in her first Winter Olympics.

Competing in her second Olympic Games, Cecilia Colledge wins the silver medal at the 1936 Winter Olympic Games.

Thomas Gregory becomes the youngest person to swim the English Channel. (Gregory completes the feat in 1988, before officials raise the age limit to 16.)

Anna Paquin nabs the Oscar for Best Supporting Actress for her role in *The Piano*.

Skateboarder Nyjah Huston becomes the youngest ever competitor at the X Games and places eighth in the "street" division of the competition. (Two years later, he will become the youngest skater to appear as a character in skating legend Tony Hawk's "Pro Skater" video game.)

Maryland bowler Richard Daff Jr. rolls a perfect 300 game.

Venetia Burney names a planet. She suggests the name Pluto (the Greek god of the underworld) for a just discovered planet. (The Lowell Observatory will make the name official.)

AGE 12

Ukrainian Sergei Karjakin earns the title of chess Grand Master from the International Chess Federation.

Jack Nicklaus routinely breaks 80 for 18 holes on the golf course.

Pocahontas saves the life of Captain John Smith, shielding his head with her body so that he will not be put to death.

Carl Wite earns a Ph.D. in mathematics from Germany's University of Giessen.

To help secure his father's release from debtors' prison, Charles Dickens quits school for a factory job—pasting labels on bottles of shoe polish.

On his twelfth birthday, David Witthoft gains national publicity for changing his shirt—his beloved Brett Favre jersey—for the first time in more than four years (1,594 consecutive days, to be precise). The shirt was a Christmas present David received when he was 7.

Franz Liszt establishes himself as a virtuoso concert pianist, performing throughout Europe. (He receives so many requests for a lock of his hair that he buys a dog and begins snipping off its fur to send to his many female admirers.)

Jesus, accompanied by parents Mary and Joseph, visits Jerusalem for Passover. While there, He astounds a group of religious leaders with His wisdom and insights.

Russian ballerina Irina Barinova wins critics' hearts for her performance in the operetta *Orpheus in the Underworld*.

AGE 13

Bill Gates writes his first computer program.

Keisha Castle-Hughes grabs an Oscar nomination (for Best Actress) for her work in *Whale Rider*.

Loretta Lynn, future country music legend, gets married.

Five-foot-nine-inch Adrian Wilson dunks a basketball, showing the jumping ability that will make him a star NFL safety—and a YouTube sensation as he shows off his 66-inch vertical jump.

Stevie Wonder records the song "Fingertips," which becomes his first No. 1 hit.

Joan of Arc reveals that she hears voices telling her to help free France from English rule.

Logan Ruffin wins three Crate/ASA Late Model Series auto races at the World Series of Asphalt, despite being the youngest driver in the field. He becomes the youngest winner in the 31-year history of the event.

Anne Frank begins her famous diary just before she and her family are forced into hiding from the Nazis.

Jodie Foster stars as a prostitute in the controversial movie *Taxi Driver*.

Seth Rogen starts performing stand-up comedy.

Future Rush drummer and lyricist Neal Peart—who skipped two grades in elementary school—begins high school.

American Marjorie Gestring wins the springboard diving gold medal at the 1936 Olympic Games in Berlin—making her the youngest athlete in any sport to earn the gold.

Already a 3-handicapper, Jack Nicklaus breaks 70 for the first time.

AGE 14

Young comedian Byron Allen begins working clubs in the Los Angeles area.

Freddy Adu becomes the youngest player in Major League Soccer history as he debuts for the D.C. United. (Two weeks later, he becomes MLS's youngest goal scorer when he puts one in the net against the MetroStars.)

"I was a 14-year-old boy
for 30 years."

— MICKEY ROONEY

Tony Hawk starts competing professionally in skateboarding.

Romanian gymnast Nadia Comaneci earns the first "perfect 10" score ever awarded in Olympic competition. (She finishes the competition with seven perfect scores.)

Brooke Shields becomes the youngest model to appear on the cover of *Vogue* magazine.

Linda Blair gives a head-turning, vomit-spewing performance in the film *The Exorcist*.

Musician Wynton Marsalis displays his trumpet skills during performances with the New Orleans Philharmonic.

Future U.S. President John Quincy Adams gets an early taste of politics, serving as secretary to the U.S. Minister to Russia.

Golfer Kimberly Kim becomes the youngest person to win the U.S. Women's Amateur Championship.

James Maxwell, nineteenth–century physicist, lectures scientists at the Royal Society at Edinburgh about his work in astronomy.

Actress Drew Barrymore pens her autobiography, *Little Girl Lost*.

Ralph Waldo Emerson enrolls at Harvard University.

Budding race car driver Joey Logano signs a development deal with the Joe Gibbs Racing organization.

AGE 15

Louis Braille begins work on a system of raised-point writing/typing, which will enable the blind to read and write.

Nepalese youngster Ming Kipa becomes the youngest person to scale Mount Everest.

Hanson Gregory, a baker's apprentice, pushes the undercooked center out of a fried bun, thereby creating the donut.

To the delight of cold ears everywhere, Chester Greenwood invents earmuffs.

Country singer Tanya Tucker appears on the cover of the rock bible, *Rolling Stone*.

"The greatest use of life
is to spend it for something
that will outlast it."

— LORD CHESTERFIELD

Alissa Geving becomes the youngest U.S. female to win a full-size sprint car race, taking the checkered flag at a 25-lap race at Petaluma Speedway.

Charlotte "Lottie" Dod wins the Wimbledon singles tennis title.

Tucker Hibbert wins the SnoCross gold medal at the Winter X Games. (Among the people Tucker defeats to win the gold is his 43-year-old father, Kirk.)

William Claiborne begins working as a congressional clerk. (He will go on to win a seat in the U.S. House of Representatives seven years later.)

Previously unknown singer/actress Demi Lovato becomes a sensation, starring in the Disney hit movie *Camp Rock* and opening for the Jonas Brothers on their concert tour.

Swimmer Dara Torres sets a world record in the 50-meter freestyle. (She will still be a world-class competitor 26 years later; see "Age 41.")

California eighth-grader Michael Avery, a 6-foot-4-inch shooting guard, accepts a scholarship offer from the University of Kentucky.

Joe Nuxhall takes the mound in a Major League Baseball game, becoming the youngest ever big-league hurler. (But it will be eight years before he pitches again.)

Sonja Henie wins the first of three Olympic figure skating gold medals.

Mary Beth Dunnichay competes in the Olympics in synchronized platform diving, making her the youngest member of the 2008 U.S. team.

AGE 16

Lauren Beeder, who survived cancer as an infant, is honored as one of the United States' Most Caring People (by the Caring Institute) for founding kidsCANCERvive, which connects young cancer patients via online support groups.

An aspiring vocalist named Ella Fitzgerald wins $25 in an amateur singing contest in Harlem.

Martina Hingis wins the Australian Open—and becomes the youngest player to be ranked No. 1 in the Women's Tennis Association. (She will hold the top spot for 80 weeks.)

Shaun White becomes the first athlete to compete in both the Summer and Winter X Games—in two different sports in the same year. At the winter event, he wins the Slopestyle and SuperPipe competitions in snowboarding and is named Best Athlete. In the summer games, he competes in skateboarding, finishing sixth in the men's vertical event.

Jordan Creel, a fullback at Alabama Christian High, runs for 232 yards to lead his team to an upset win over Daleville. Creel plays the game in honor of his mother, Karen, who was killed in a fire the day before.

Swimmer Michael Phelps breaks the world record in the 200-meter butterfly event, making him the youngest male swimmer to hold a world mark.

Skinny Angelo Siciliano sees a statue of Hercules at the Brooklyn Museum, which inspires him to join his local YMCA and start pumping iron. The workouts pay off, as Angelo becomes a famous bodybuilder and fitness guru. (He later changes his name to Charles Atlas.)

Fresh off a strong performance at the 2008 Olympics, gymnast Shawn Johnson leads the Pledge of Allegiance at the Democratic National Convention. (Johnson won four Olympic medals, including a gold in the balance beam.)

"From what we get, we can make a living; what we give, however, makes a life."

— ARTHUR ASHE

Arthur de Lulli composes "The Celebrated Chop Waltz," which will soon become known by its shorter moniker, "Chopsticks."

Unseeded Coco Vandeweghe wins the 2008 U.S. Open girls' championship, marking the first time in 13 years that an American girl has won the title. (Vandeweghe is the niece of former NBA star Kiki Vandeweghe.)

Patty Duke gets the Best Actress Oscar, portraying Helen Keller in *The Miracle Worker*.

Tracy Austin wins the U.S. Open Tennis championship.

Buddha marries Yasodhara, his princess cousin, who is also 16.

Courtney Rayle wins her age division in the seventy-first Soap Box Derby, as female competitors capture five of the six championship trophies.

Danica Patrick drops out of high school to race Indy-style cars overseas in England's Formula Vauxhall series.

AGE 17

High school junior Bonnie Richardson single-handedly wins the Texas Class 1A team track-and-field championship. The only athlete from her school to qualify for the state meet, Richardson wins the high jump and 200 meters, places second in the long jump and 100 meters, and takes third in the discus throw.

Singer/songwriter Taylor Swift captures the Country Music Association's Horizon Award honoring the genre's most promising emerging star.

Serena Williams becomes the first African-American since Arthur Ashe to win a Grand Slam singles title when she rules the 1999 U.S. Open.

Donny Robinson leaves the world of musical theater to compete in BMX bike racing. The change agrees with him; he makes the 2008 U.S. Olympic team.

Tom Morris Jr. wins the British Open golf championship.

German Boris "Boom Boom" Becker wins the Wimbledon singles tennis title.

Judy Garland stars as Dorothy in the classic film *The Wizard of Oz*.

In a crucial Hundred Years' War victory, French army captain Joan of Arc leads her troops against the English, forcing them to withdraw from Orleans.

Pele scores six times in the final three games to lead Brazil to its first World Cup soccer championship.

Harry Houdini makes his debut as a professional magician.

All-around athlete Bob Mathias wins the grueling Olympic decathlon. (He will win it again four years later.)

Bangladesh's Dolly Akter is recognized by *Time for Kids* magazine for her work with UNICEF in helping her country's citizens learn the importance of safe water for drinking and bathing.

Kansas distance ace Jim Ryun becomes the first high school runner to break the four-minute mile.

Marco Polo begins his famous 24-year expedition of Asia.

AGE 18

The top pick in the 2007 National Hockey League draft, Patrick Kane (all 163 pounds of him) begins his pro career for the Chicago Blackhawks.

Mick Jagger debuts with his new rock band, the Rollin' Stones. (The band will add the "g" eventually.)

Striker Jozy Altidore makes his debut with the U.S. national soccer team on the heels of a Major League Soccer season in which the New Jersey teen tallied nine goals in 22 games for the New York Red Bulls.

Writer William Shakespeare marries Anne Hathaway, eight years his senior.

Ken Rosewall wins the Australian Open, playing in his home country.

Jesse James commits his first bank robbery.

Jennifer Beals stars as a welder and a dancer in *Flashdance*.

Cassius Clay (later to be known as Muhammad Ali) wins the light heavyweight boxing gold medal at the 1960 Olympic Games in Rome.

Comedian Byron Allen makes his TV debut on *The Tonight Show*, becoming the show's youngest comic to date.

Jake Deitchler beats two more experienced opponents to become the first high school wrestler in 28 years to make the U.S. Olympic team—and the youngest Greco-Roman grappler ever to earn a spot on a U.S. squad.

Al Kaline signs a $30,000 bonus-salary agreement with the Detroit Tigers, where he will spend his entire baseball career.

Mary Shelley starts penning the tale of Dr. Frankenstein and his monster.

NASCAR driver Joey Logano wins his first Nationwide Series race in only his third career start.

Tommy Hilfiger opens his first clothing store, selling— among other things—bell-bottom pants.

Gymnast Nastia Liukin takes the all-around gold medal at the 2008 Olympics. The second-place finish by her friend and teammate Shawn Johnson, 16, marks the first time two American gymnasts finish first and second in an Olympic all-around.

AGE 19

At the 1956 Olympic Games, Al Oerter wins the first of his four gold medals in the discus throw, breaking the Olympic record by more than four feet on his first toss.

Barbra Streisand earns rave reviews as she opens in Broadway's *I Can Get It for You Wholesale*.

Russian math student Nikolaj Sazhin wins the light heavy-weight World Chessboxing Championship. (In chessboxing, competitors alternate three-minute boxing rounds with four-minute rounds of speed chess. Victory can come via either a knockout or a checkmate.)

William Hanna, along with his partner Joe Barbera, creates the cartoon characters Tom and Jerry.

One-hundred-fifteen-pound college student Kate Stelnick becomes the first person to eat the Ye Old 96er burger at Denny's Beer Barrel Pub in Clearfield, Pennsylvania. Consuming the 6-pound burger (and its 5 pounds of condiments) takes Kate 2 hours and 54 minutes, just under the 3-hour time limit.

Golfer John J. McDermott wins the 1911 U.S. Open.

Jack Nicklaus wins the first of his two U.S. Amateur golf titles.

Sidney Crosby wins the National Hockey League scoring title, as well as the Hart Memorial Trophy, given to the NHL's most valuable player.

Golfer Inbee Park defeats a stellar field, including Annika Sorenstam and Lorena Ochoa, to win the 2008 U.S. Open—and $560,000.

Working from his dorm room at Harvard University, Mark Zuckerberg launches Facebook, a social networking site that soon grows to more than 70 million active users and is valued at $15 billion.

Gavrilo Princip assassinates Austrian Archduke Ferdinand, an act that helps spark World War I.

Graham Rahal wins his IndyCar Series debut race—the Grand Prix of St. Petersburg—becoming the youngest winner in major open-wheel racing history. (Graham is the son of racing great Bobby Rahal.)

Marie Antoinette assumes the role of France's queen.

Kelly Slater becomes the youngest ever world surfing champion. (He will go on to win seven more world titles.)

Bob Marley forms the reggae group The Wailing Wailers.

AGE 20

Olympic decathlete Rafer Johnson, competing with an injured knee, pulls a stomach muscle warming up for his first event but still goes on to win the silver medal at the 1956 games in Melbourne, Australia. (Four years later, in Rome, he will win the gold.)

Detroit Tiger Al Kaline, all 150 pounds of him, wins the American League batting title.

Timothy Hutton wins the Best Supporting Actor Oscar for *Ordinary People*.

Andrew Fisher a Nebraska-based Web designer, uses eBay to auction off his forehead as advertising space. He receives $37,375 to display the logo for a snoring remedy for 30 days.

Frenchman Henri Cornet wins the Tour de France (after the four riders who finished ahead of him are disqualified).

Gene Sarazen wins the 1922 PGA Championship.

Ji-Yai Shin of South Korea becomes the youngest ever winner of the Women's British Open.

Rookie Magic Johnson leads the Los Angeles Lakers to an NBA title and is named Finals MVP, despite being too young to legally indulge in any of the celebratory locker room champagne.

Alexander the Great becomes King of Macedonia and leads the Greeks into war against Persia.

San Diego State pitcher Stephen Strasburg strikes out 23 University of Utah hitters in one game. (Strasburg will go on to become the only collegian to make the United States' 2008 Olympic baseball team.)

20th Century-Fox Studios offers an acting contract to Norma Jean Mortensen. Young Norma Jean also gets something else from the studio—a new name: Marilyn Monroe.

Julie Andrews, playing Eliza Doolittle, thrills audiences in the Broadway production of *My Fair Lady*.

Kathy Switzer becomes the first woman to compete in the Boston Marathon—in 1967, five years before women are allowed to run in the prestigious race. (She enters the race as "K.W. Switzer," so her application raises no suspicion.) Switzer finishes the race—despite the race director's attempts to pull her off the course—after her boyfriend shoves the director out of the way.

AGE 21

Nathan Hale, a key figure in the American Revolution, is captured by the British and executed. He is quoted as saying, "I regret that I have but one life to lose for my country."

Two years after undergoing a heart procedure called a cardiac ablation to correct a rapid heartbeat, U.S. swimmer Rebecca Soni wins a gold medal in the 200-meter breaststroke at the 2008 Olympics. She races to a new world record and beats former record holder Australia's Leisel Jones by almost two seconds.

Orlando Magic star Dwight Howard becomes the youngest player in NBA history to collect 3,000 career rebounds.

At the 2008 Olympic Games, Henry Cejudo becomes the United States' youngest Olympic wrestling champion. (He won the national freestyle championship while still a high school student.)

At the 2008 Summer Paralympic Games, Oscar Pistorius takes the gold medals in the 100-, 200-, and 400-meter sprints.

Running with blade-like prosthetics, Oscar Pistorius, who had both of his lower legs amputated at age 1, sprints 400 meters in an eye-popping 46.25 seconds, missing a chance to qualify for the South African 4x400-meter Olympic relay team by a mere 7/10 of a second.

Steve Jobs introduces the Apple computer, created with young colleague Steve Wozniak.

Tiger Woods becomes the youngest golfer to win the Masters.

Maya Lin, a Yale undergraduate student, wins a competition to design the Vietnam Veterans Memorial in Washington, D.C.

Chinese high hurdler Liu Xiang becomes the only male track Olympic gold medalist in his country's history, making him a national hero to 1.3 billion people.

Upon her marriage to U.S. President Grover Cleveland, Frances Cleveland becomes the country's youngest First Lady. Seven years later, she gives birth to Esther Cleveland, the only child ever born to a First Lady in the White House.

Elvis Presley records "Heartbreak Hotel."

Jane Austen completes a novel called *Pride and Prejudice*—which will take 16 years to get published.

In less than half a day, all-around athlete Babe Didrikson breaks four track-and-field world records.

Jamaican sprinter Usain Bolt bolts to two Olympic gold medals—and two world records—in the 100 and 200 meters at the 2008 Olympics. (He'll later add a third gold, in the 4 x100-meter relay.)

AGE 22

Making his marathon debut in New York City, Alberto Salazar wins the prestigious race, covering the 26.2 miles in 2 hours, 9 minutes, and 41 seconds, setting a new course record and defeating the reigning record holder, Bill Rodgers.

Charles Darwin launches his famed five-year voyage on the H.M.S. Beagle.

Rafael Nadal ends Roger Federer's streak of five straight Wimbledon championships in a 2008 classic five-set tennis marathon that lasts almost five hours.

Six-foot-three-inch softball pitcher Monica Abbott sets a Division 1 record for strikeouts—724 during her senior season.

Artist Norman Rockwell sells his first *Saturday Evening Post* cover.

Contrary to Constitutional rules (which set the minimum age for U.S. Representatives at 25), William Claiborne, already a member of the Tennessee Supreme Court, wins a seat in the U.S. House of Representatives.

Swimmer Mark Spitz wins seven gold medals—and sets seven world records—at the 1972 Olympic Games.

Dick Clark premieres his new TV show, which he calls *American Bandstand*.

AGE 23

For her heroism in the Iraq war, Leigh Ann Hester, a sergeant in the Kentucky National Guard, earns the Silver Star for exceptional valor, becoming the first woman to receive the honor for an offensive action against an enemy.

English poet John Keats enjoys one of the most creative years of his life, writing "Ode to a Grecian Urn," "Ode to a Nightingale," "To Autumn," "Ode to Melancholy," and "The Eve of St. Agnes," among others.

Milwaukee first baseman Prince Fielder becomes the youngest Major League player ever to hit 50 home runs in a season.

Roger Peckinpaugh serves as interim manager of the New York Yankees (for 17 games).

The skinny, 6-foot-1-inch Joey Chestnut wolfs 66 Nathan's Famous hot dogs in 12 minutes to win the world hot-dog-eating championship.

Musician Jerry Garcia founds a group called The Grateful Dead.

Annie Liebovitz is named chief photographer for *Rolling Stone* magazine, a job that will launch her as the country's best-known portrait photographer.

Tom Monaghan creates a pizza delivery chain he calls Domino's.

John Travolta stars as disco-dancing Tony Manero in *Saturday Night Fever*.

Jane Taylor pens a nursery rhyme called "Twinkle, Twinkle, Little Star."

At the 2008 Olympics, swimmer Michael Phelps wins eight gold medals, the most ever by an athlete in Olympic history. He sets seven world records in the process, then signs a $1.6 million book deal to tell his life's story.

AGE 24

Four years after a car crash that injured her and killed her brother, Polish swimmer Otylia Jedrzejczak sets a world record in the 200-meter butterfly.

Despite competing with testicular cancer, swimmer Eric Shanteau qualifies for the U.S. Olympic team in the 200-meter breaststroke.

Four years after quitting the sport of cycling—and selling her gear on eBay—Sarah Hammer makes a comeback and wins two straight world individual pursuit titles.

Former *American Idol* contestant Carrie Underwood wins her second straight Country Music Association Female Vocalist of the Year Award.

Focusing on mechanics rather than power, diminutive pitcher Tim Lincecum—the 1,261st player selected in the 2005 draft—becomes a Major League pitching sensation. The

5-foot-10-inch, 172-pound San Francisco Giants hurler throws a 98-mph fastball and leads the Majors in strikeouts.

Philippe Petit gains worldwide notoriety when he walks between New York's Twin Towers on a wire cable suspended 1,350 feet above the ground. (After successfully completing the unsanctioned stunt, which takes almost an hour to complete, he is arrested and later placed in a psychological counseling program.)

South African swimmer Natalie du Toit becomes the first paralympian to compete in the Olympics (in the 10-kilometer open-water race). Du Toit, who had her lower left leg amputated after her scooter was struck by a car, qualifies for the Beijing Olympics by finishing fourth in the 2008 open-water world championships. At the games, she finishes a respectable sixteenth.

At the request of George Washington, Betsy Ross sews the first American flag.

Cleveland Browns wide receiver Braylon Edwards pledges $1 million in college scholarships for 100 local eighth-grade students—if they maintain a 2.5 GPA, do community service work, and attend academic and life-skills workshops.

James Dean stars in the movie *East of Eden*.

Flying an experimental rocket plane, pilot Chuck Yeager becomes the first person to break the sound barrier.

AGE 25

Kelly Pavlik, a decided underdog, knocks out Jermain Taylor to win the undisputed middleweight boxing title and improve his record to 32-0, with a knockout percentage of better than 90 percent.

Reggie Love transitions from professional football to serve as personal aide to Democratic presidential nominee Barack Obama.

Orson Welles writes, directs, produces, and stars in the classic film *Citizen Kane*.

Softball pitcher Cat Osterman leads the United States to its third straight gold medal at the 2004 Olympics. Her earned-run average: 0.0.

Scientist Werner Heisenberg unveils his famous "uncertainty principle."

Soviet cosmonaut Gherman Titov becomes the youngest human in space when his Vostok 2 spacecraft is launched in 1961.

Schoolteacher John Scopes explains evolution to his students, an act that will lead to the famous "Monkey Trial."

Ryan Hall runs the second half of a marathon faster than the first half to win the 2008 U.S. Olympic trials in a record time of 2:09:02.

In his famous plane Spirit of St. Louis, Charles Lindbergh becomes the first person to fly solo across the Atlantic.

Writer Roger Ebert becomes film critic for the *Chicago Sun-Times*.

English distance runner Roger Bannister becomes the first person to break the four-minute mile.

Pablo Picasso paints *Les Demoiselles d'Avignon*, ushering in the age of Modern Art.

Vivien Leigh plays Scarlett O'Hara in the film *Gone With the Wind*.

French swimmer Alain "The Hovercraft" Bernard sets world records in the 50- and 100-meter races in a single meet.

AGE 26

The first woman in space, Valentina Vladimirova Tereshkova, orbits the earth six times.

Albert Einstein proposes his theory of relativity.

Ski jumper Chuck Ryan soars 150 feet in a competition—without his skis, due to equipment malfunction. He lands safely, using a baseball-style slide.

Joltin' Joe DiMaggio collects base hits in 56 consecutive games.

Brandt Snedeker, an older-than-usual rookie on the PGA Tour, wins his first tour event at the 2007 Wyndham Championships.

Brad Walker clears 19' 9¾" to set a new U.S. record in the pole vault. Walker's vault is also the world's best in the past seven years.

Michelangelo completes the sculpture he calls *Pieta*.

After months and months serving as tabloid fodder, Britney Spears gains a measure of revenge at the 2008 Video Music Awards when she collects awards for Video of the Year, Best Female Video, and Best Pop Video.

Jimi Hendrix performs his famous "Star-Spangled Banner" finale at the Woodstock Music Festival.

After two injury-plagued seasons, Chicago Cubs pitcher Rich Harden tops the Major Leagues in earned run average and leads his team into the playoffs.

When his World War II PT boat is sunk by a Japanese destroyer, future U.S. President John F. Kennedy helps several of his fellow crew members reach shore safely.

AGE 27

Elias Howe invents the sewing machine.

Charles Schulz creates a comic strip he dubs "Peanuts."

To cheer up a sick child, Beatrix Potter writes and illustrates a story about a rabbit named Peter.

"The future is purchased
by the present."

– SAMUEL JOHNSON

Roger Federer wins his fifth consecutive U.S. Open tennis championship and comes within one major title (13) of tying Pete Sampras for the all-time record.

Using radio waves, Guglielmo Marconi sends the first transatlantic message.

After playing softball for the U.S. Olympic team, left fielder Jessica Mendoza leaves competition to become president of the Women's Sports Foundation.

Australian Robbie Madison breaks the world motorcycle-jumping record, soaring 322 feet. ESPN televises the event live. (Madison will later extend his mark to 351 feet.)

Actor Adam West makes his debut as TV's Batman.

Hugh Hefner starts a magazine he calls *Playboy*.

Steven Spielberg directs a movie called *Jaws*, starring Richard Dreyfuss, Robert Shaw, Roy Scheider, and a mechanical shark.

Ingrid Bergman stars as Ilsa—opposite Humphrey Bogart—in *Casablanca*.

A year after being banished from the U.S. soccer team, goal-keeper Hope Solo returns to the squad and leads them to a gold medal at the 2008 Olympics. (The U.S. shuts out Brazil 1-0 in the championship match.)

AGE 28

Contrary to Constitutional rules (which set the minimum age for U.S. senators at 30), Tennessee Republican John Eaton is sworn into office.

Golfing great Bobby Jones retires from the game he has dominated. (But with college degrees in English lit, engineering, and law, he has plenty of options for life after golf.)

Washington Post reporter Carl Bernstein begins investigating a politically motivated break-in at the Watergate Hotel.

F. Scott Fitzgerald publishes his famed novel *The Great Gatsby*.

After failing three times to make the U.S. Olympic team—never finishing higher than eighth in any qualifying race—Mark Warkentin finally makes the team in 2008, as his country's only competitor in the 10-kilometer open swim. He finishes eighth overall, just 21 seconds behind the gold medalist.

Julie Andrews stars as Maria von Trapp in *The Sound of Music*.

Bob Keeshan makes his debut as a character known as Captain Kangaroo.

Golfer Sergio Garcia takes a big step to shed his identity as "the best player never to have won a major" when he wins his first Players Championship, known as the PGA Tour's "fifth major." Garcia's victory, which comes after a sudden-death playoff, breaks a 53-event winless streak.

Albert Camus publishes *The Stranger*.

African-American Jackie Robinson plays his first game for the Brooklyn Dodgers, breaking Major League Baseball's color barrier.

U.S. decathlete Bryan Clay lays claim to the title of World's Greatest Athlete as he wins the gold medal at the 2008 Olympics in Beijing.

AGE 29

Alexander Graham Bell invents the telephone.

Filipino boxer Manny Pacquiao knocks out David Diaz to win the WBC lightweight title, becoming the first Asian fighter to win title belts in four weight classes.

Edvard Munch paints *The Scream*.

Kobe Bryant scores the 20,000th point of his NBA career, making him the youngest player to reach that milestone (beating former record holder Wilt Chamberlain by 12 days).

Jennifer Michel, the men's and women's cross-country coach at Western State College, becomes the first woman to be named national men's coach of the year—in any of the NCAA's divisions. In her first year as coach, she leads the Mountaineers to a North Central Region championship and a second-place finish in the NCAA Division II nationals.

Former slave Harriet Tubman begins freeing slaves via the Underground Railroad. On the 19 trips she conducts, more than 300 slaves make it safely to the northern U.S. or Canada.

J. Edgar Hoover is named Director of the FBI, a post he will hold for 48 years (until his death).

Berry Gordy founds Motown Records.

Emily Dickinson withdraws from society to focus on writing poetry.

AGE 30

Matthew Brown, a left-leg-below-the-knee amputee, wins a gold medal in the discus with a toss of 154 feet 9 inches at the Parapan American Games. A high school football and track coach, Brown also takes a bronze medal in the shot put.

Sylvia Plath sees her lone novel, *The Bell Jar*, published. (She commits suicide a month later.)

Actor Sylvester Stallone stars in *Rocky*, a film he also wrote.

Three years after retiring from competition, Kelly Slater returns to surfing and wins his eighth world championship—becoming the oldest competitor to hold the title.

Thomas Edison invents the phonograph player.

Golfer Nancy Lopez is inducted into the LPGA Hall of Fame.

Tiger Woods becomes the youngest player to amass 50 PGA Tour wins.

Kerri Walsh (along with partner Misty May-Treanor) captures a second straight beach volleyball Olympic gold medal. (In the process, the duo extends their year-long streak without a loss to 108 matches. The streak will eventually end at 112.)

AGE 31

Four-time WNBA all-star Becky Hammon becomes a naturalized Russian citizen so that she can compete in the 2008 Olympics. She leads her team to the bronze medal.

Bill Gates makes his first billion dollars.

Tennis great Pete Sampras wins his fourteenth, and final, major title at the U.S. Open.

Working with her husband, Marie Curie discovers radium.

Martine Clement wrecks while bicycling to a half-marathon race. She completes the 13.1-mile race, then discovers that she has broken both arms in the wreck.

Ralph Nader publishes his whistle-blowing book about the auto industry, *Unsafe at Any Speed*.

Considered one of the greatest writers of all time, William Shakespeare's surviving works include 38 plays, 154 sonnets, and numerous other poems.

William Shakespeare pens *Romeo and Juliet*.

Country star Loretta Lynn becomes a grandma.

Chuck Berry records the song "Johnny B. Goode," which *Rolling Stone* will one day name The Greatest Guitar Song of All Time.

Rami Zur makes it to the semifinals of the 2008 Olympic 500-meter kayak singles competition—a remarkable feat considering he broke a bone in his neck after competing in the 2004 games. (Zur returned to training just five months after surgery.)

Charles Dickens publishes *A Christmas Carol*.

Athlete Breaux Greer leads a double life—qualifying for the 2008 Olympics in the javelin and starring as the character Hurricane on the TV show *American Gladiators*.

AGE 32

After a 54-home-run 2007 season, Alex Rodriguez wins his second American League Most Valuable Player Award in two years.

J.D. Salinger publishes *Catcher in the Rye*.

Army staff sergeant Christopher Downs becomes the oldest boxer ever to compete for the U.S. Olympic team.

Harold Ross founds *The New Yorker* magazine.

Lane Kiffin takes on the head coaching duties of the Oakland Raiders—making him the youngest head coach in any of the four major sports.

Sharon Stone becomes the talk of the entertainment world for her controversial role in the film *Basic Instinct*.

Lila Wallace, along with husband DeWitt, founds *Reader's Digest*.

With her six-day flight in the Challenger space shuttle, Sally Ride becomes the first American woman in space.

Sydney Pollack earns the first of his many Oscar nominations for Best Director for the film *They Shoot Horses, Don't They?*

Ali MacGraw costars with Ryan O'Neal in *Love Story*.

AGE 33

Russia's Bouvaisa Saitiev wins his third Olympic gold medal in wrestling at the 2008 Games. (He won his first gold when he was just 21.)

Running her first marathon in more than two years, Paula Radcliffe wins the New York City Marathon in 2:23:09. The win marks Radcliffe's seventh win in eight marathons. Radcliffe's long layoff was due to the birth of her daughter and a stress fracture in her lower back.

Eight years after suffering a career-threatening herniated disc, weight lifter Melanie Roach makes her first Olympic team. The mother of three can lift more than twice her 117-pound body weight in the clean and jerk. She finishes a respectable sixth at the Beijing Games.

Carolina Panther Jake Delhomme becomes just the second quarterback in NFL history to make a full recovery from "Tommy John" elbow surgery and return to the field.

Thomas Jefferson pens the Declaration of Independence.

George Lucas creates a film called *Star Wars*.

"One who stops being better
stops being good."

— Oliver Cromwell

Greco-Roman wrestler T. C. Dantzler creates TC logicQ, a background-screening company. (He will require time off from his firm when he makes the U.S. Olympic team in 2008.)

Religious reformer Martin Luther nails his famous 95 Theses on the door of the Wittenberg Cathedral.

Phil Knight launches a shoe and apparel company that he calls Nike.

Spain's Carlos Sastre wins the 2008 Tour de France, edging out riders from Austria and Australia in the second-closest finish in the race's 105-year history.

Delano Meriwether earns notability on two fronts: competing as a world-class sprinter and serving as a physician for the Department of Health, Education and Welfare—who is called on to consult President Gerald Ford on protecting Americans against the swine flu.

Stay-at-home dad Michael Thompson wins $1 million in a fantasy fishing contest.

At the 2008 Beijing Games, gymnast Oksana Chusovitina competes in her fifth Olympics—for her third different country. She makes the finals in the vault competition, where the average age of the other seven finalists is 19.

AGE 34

Harper Lee writes the novel *To Kill a Mockingbird*.

Haile Gebrselassie wins the 2007 Berlin Marathon in a world-record time of 2:04:26, slicing an amazing 29 seconds off the old mark. The Ethiopian runner averages under 4 minutes and 45 seconds per mile.

Amelia Earhart becomes the first woman to fly solo across the Atlantic.

Martin Luther King Jr. delivers his famous "I Have a Dream" speech.

Point guard Jason Kidd joins Oscar Robertson and Magic Johnson as the only players to average more than nine assists and eight rebounds in a single season.

Country music star Gretchen Wilson earns her General Education Development (GED) diploma. She celebrates her graduation ceremony the same month that her daughter Grace, age 7, finishes first grade. "I don't want [Grace] to think you can be this successful without an education," Wilson says.

"We must learn to live together like brothers and sisters, or we will perish together like fools."

– MARTIN LUTHER KING JR.

In a poll of fellow National Hockey League players, Anaheim defenseman Scott Niedermayer is voted the second-best skater in the league. The average age of the other top five vote getters: 23.

Kindergarten teacher Mildred Hill composes the music for a ditty called "Happy Birthday to You."

Sixteen years after competing in her first Olympics, judo expert Valerie Gotay wins the 126-pound division in the 2008 Olympic trials. A mother of two, Gotay had previously retired from competition for eleven years.

Daniel Boone opens the door to the American West by blazing a trail through the Cumberland Gap.

Aging Green Bay Packers backup wide receiver Max McGee is unexpectedly forced into action in the first Super Bowl. He responds with seven catches for 138 yards and two touchdowns—including the first TD in Super Bowl history—as the Packers win.

AGE 35

Tony Bennett records his biggest hit song, "I Left My Heart in San Francisco."

In just six weeks, Louisa May Alcott writes *Little Women*.

Francis Scott Key writes an anthem titled "The Star-Spangled Banner."

William Shatner makes his debut as Captain Kirk on the TV show *Star Trek*.

Jason Richko, a resort property manager, wins the 2007 U.S. Amateur Billiard Championships, improving on his twenty-fifth-place finish the year before.

Disguised as a male, Joan Anglicus becomes the only female Pope (dubbed John VIII). Her reign as Pope ends two and a half years later when she gives birth—during a public ceremony.

Svetlana Savitskaya becomes the first woman to walk in space.

Audrey Hepburn stars as Eliza Doolittle in the film version of *My Fair Lady*.

Self-proclaimed "fantasy football widow" Allison Lodish (whose husband belongs to 10 fantasy football leagues) gains national publicity after forming WAFS—Women Against Fantasy Sports. The organization's Web site features a message board for members to post their laments and stories—and also sells merchandise, such as panties with mottoes like CLOSED FOR THE FANTASY SEASON.

Margret Rey writes a children's book called *Curious George*.

AGE 36

Kurt Warner, thought by many to be washed up, takes over for struggling young quarterback Matt Leinart to run the offense for the Arizona Cardinals.

Though officially retired from tennis for four years, Pete Sampras defeats the virtually invincible Roger Federer, the world's No. 1-ranked player, in an exhibition match, 7-6, 6-4. (Federer had won three of four Grand Slam events during the previous season.)

Albert Einstein proclaims his general theory of relativity; the fields of physics and astronomy will never be the same.

Ekaterina Karsten, a rower from Belarus, becomes just the sixth woman to win medals in five Summer Olympic Games.

Only six years after retiring, Dodger pitching great Sandy Koufax is elected to the Baseball Hall of Fame, making him the youngest member of the elite fraternity.

Johnny Carson debuts as host of *The Tonight Show*.

Ben Franklin invents the Franklin stove.

English Quaker leader William Penn founds Pennsylvania.

AGE 37

Five years after his Pro Bowl heyday with the San Francisco 49ers, Jeff Garcia wins the starting quarterback position for the Tampa Bay Buccaneers and leads the team to an 8-6 record, throwing 13 touchdown passes and only 4 interceptions.

England's King James I commissions an English translation of the Bible.

Mike Modano of the Dallas Stars breaks the National Hockey League's all-time record for points scored by a U.S.-born player.

Ann Landers begins a newspaper advice column.

Greco-Roman wrestler T. C. Dantzler qualifies (in 2008) for his first Olympics. Despite making the world Greco-Roman team five times and winning the U.S. Olympic trials in 2004, he had never qualified for the Games in his weight class.

Amy Tan publishes *The Joy Luck Club*.

Joe Sakic becomes the second-oldest NHL player to record a 100-point season, displaying the same skate speed, rink vision, and deft passing he showcased as a 19-year-old rookie.

Giacomo Puccini premieres his opera *La Boheme* in Turin, Italy.

AGE 38

Dr. Jonas Salk develops a vaccine for polio.

Finland's Tommi Huotari, with a toss of 294 feet, wins the world cell phone-throwing championships. (Huotari moved to the cell phone competition after tossing potatoes successfully.)

Neil Armstrong becomes the first person to walk on the moon.

"That's one small step for man, one giant leap for mankind."

– NEIL ARMSTRONG

Coco Chanel unveils her perfume, Chanel No. 5.

After making a fortune as an attorney and film studio executive, Kathy Goodman leaves those high-powered worlds to teach English and social studies at a high school in Van Nuys, California.

After missing the cut at the 1968 Masters and finishing fifty-ninth at the U.S. Open, Arnold Palmer silences his critics—and snaps an eight-month losing streak—by firing a final round 67 to overcome a three-stroke deficit and win the Kemper Open. In the process, he becomes the first golfer to top $1 million in career earnings.

Grant Wood completes a painting he titles *American Gothic*.

Green Bay Packer Brett Favre becomes the National Football League's all-time leader in touchdown passes.

Feminist Gloria Steinem co-founds and becomes editor of *Ms. Magazine*.

Cincinnati Red Ken Griffey Jr. hits his 600th home run.

Mother Teresa founds the Missionaries of Charity Sisterhood.

Cesar Chavez organizes California grape pickers in a historic and effective strike for better pay and working conditions.

"I know God will not
give me anything I cannot
handle. I just wish He didn't
trust me so much."

– MOTHER TERESA

"It is hard to fail,
but it is worse never to
have tried to succeed."

— TEDDY ROOSEVELT

AGE 39

Lao-tzu founds a belief system known as Taoism.

Kenny Chesney wins his third Country Music Association Male Vocalist of the Year Award.

Author/illustrator Dorothy Kunhardt completes work on a tactile kids' book titled *Pat the Bunny*.

After 16 seasons, Mike Piazza retires as the best-hitting catcher in Major League Baseball history. Drafted 1,309th by the Los Angeles Dodgers, Piazza went on to hit 427 career home runs, and his 396 homers as a catcher set a new MLB record. Befitting his quiet style, he retires via a press release, not a giant media event.

After dropping 70 pounds, Jean Nidetch creates a movement called Weight Watchers.

During the Spanish-American War, future President Teddy Roosevelt leads his Rough Riders in their charge up San Juan Hill.

At the 2008 Beijing Olympics, pentathlete Sheila Taormina becomes the first woman to compete in three different sports in the Olympics. She represented the U.S. in swimming in 1996 (winning a gold medal) and as a triathlete in 2000 and 2004. Only three years before the Beijing Games, Taormina had never participated in three of the pentathlon's five events—fencing, target shooting, and equestrian. (The other two events are swimming and running.)

Portuguese explorer Ferdinand Magellan begins his historic circumnavigation of the globe.

Bing Crosby records "White Christmas."

Comedian/actress Ellen DeGeneres comes out of the closet.

Race car driver Janet Guthrie becomes the first woman to compete in the Indianapolis 500.

Frenchman Stephane Rousson logs four hours of flying time over the coastal town of Toulon, via a blimp whose two 10-foot propellers are powered by a recumbent bike hanging from the blimp's belly. (Rousson's ultimate goal is to complete a 5½ hour, 34-mile flight across the English Channel.)

AGE 40

After failing to make the U.S. Olympic teams in 2000 and 2004, pole vaulter Jeff Hartwig earns a spot in the 2008 Olympic Games, becoming the oldest American vaulter in Olympic history. At the games, he clears a respectable 18 feet 2½ inches but doesn't qualify for the finals.

A year after enduring abdominal surgery for cancer, Babe Didrikson Zaharias wins five golf tournaments during 1954, including her third U.S. Women's Open.

Susan Sarandon stars in *Bull Durham* and meets future love Tim Robbins.

Harriet Beecher Stowe publishes *Uncle Tom's Cabin*.

While playing golf on his fortieth birthday, John Elway hits a hole in one.

The seemingly ageless Warren Moon quarterbacks the Seattle Seahawks to a respectable 7-7 record, tossing 25 touchdown passes along the way.
Hammerin' Hank Aaron hits his 715th home run, surpassing Babe Ruth's all-time record.

Leo Tolstoy finishes writing a mammoth novel he titles *War and Peace*.

Recovering alcoholic Bill Wilson cofounds Alcoholics Anonymous.

Mark Twain publishes his novel *The Adventures of Tom Sawyer*.

Lucille Ball debuts as Lucy Ricardo in the TV comedy *I Love Lucy*.

Inventor King Gillette begins developing a disposable multiblade razor, a process that will take him several years to complete.

AGE 41

The oldest punter in the NFL, Jeff Feagles is named by his fellow players as one of the league's top five punters.

Al Jolson stars in *The Jazz Singer*, the first major motion picture "talkie."

"The secret of staying young is to live honestly, eat slowly, and lie about your age."

– LUCILLE BALL

Dara Torres earns a spot on the Olympic team during the 2008 U.S. Swimming Olympic trials—setting an American record in the 50-meter freestyle in the process. Torres, who came out of retirement for a third time to compete in the 2008 trials, becomes the oldest American swimmer to make an Olympic team—and the first to make five teams. She wins three silver medals at the 2008 Games.

William Shakespeare writes *King Lear*.

Sue Grafton writes *A Is for Alibi*, the first of her alphabetical mystery-novel series.

AGE 42

Rosa Parks refuses to give up her seat on a Birmingham, Alabama, bus, becoming a symbol in the battle for racial equality.

After the assassination of President McKinley, Teddy Roosevelt becomes the youngest ever President of the United States.

Humphrey Bogart stars as Rick, opposite Ingrid Bergman, in the film *Casablanca*.

"One person with courage
makes a majority."

— ANDREW JACKSON

L. Ron Hubbard founds the Church of Scientology.

A man apparently not afraid to seek guidance for direction, **Galileo Galilei** invents the compass.

Margot Fonteyn earns 23 curtain calls when she dances for the first time with a new partner, 24-year-old Rudolph Nureyev, at London's Covent Garden.

Woody Allen cowrites, directs, and stars in the film *Annie Hall*.

An Austrian abbot named **Gregor Mendel** publishes findings about his experiments in heredity, making him a pioneer in the field of genetics.

AGE 43

In the wake of a battle with colon cancer, **Babe Didrikson** wins her third U.S. Open golf championship by 12 strokes over her nearest competitor.

Dr. Benjamin Spock publishes his *Common Sense Book of Baby and Child Care*, which will go on to become one of the best-selling books of all time.

Just a month shy of his forty-fourth birthday, Vinny Testaverde reenters the National Football League and become's the league's oldest quarterback to start—and win—a game, leading the Carolina Panthers to victory over the Arizona Cardinals and their 36-year-old QB, Kurt Warner.

Mixed-martial artist Randy Couture comes out of retirement to win the Ultimate Fighting Championship's heavyweight title, decisively defeating Tim Sylvia, who stands half a foot taller than Couture and outweighs him by more than 40 pounds.

Physician John H. Kellogg creates a flaked breakfast cereal.

Anna Edson Taylor rides a barrel off Niagara Falls—and becomes the first person to survive the feat.

Inventor Tory Weber unveils the Terma Blade, a hockey skate with a battery-warmed blade. Weber says the melted ice surrounding the blade reduces friction and increases skaters' speed, thereby reducing exertion and lowering heart rates.

Susan von der Lippe competes in the 2008 U.S. Swimming Olympic trials as the oldest athlete, male or female, in the field.

"Our greatest glory
is not in never failing,
but in rising
every time we fall."

— CONFUCIUS

AGE 44

After having the lower part of his right leg amputated due to a cancerous cyst, award-winning jazz bass guitarist Wayman Tisdale tours in support of his latest album, *Rebound*, which was inspired by his fight against cancer. (Before embarking on his career as a musician, Tisdale was a star in the NBA.)

Just before the start of the 2008 NFL season, placekicker John Carney—recently cast off by the Kansas City Chiefs and the Jacksonville Jaguars—signs a deal with the New York Giants, the defending Super Bowl Champions. In the season opener, he nails three of three field goals.

Ageless boxer Evander Holyfield fights for the WBO heavyweight championship. Though he loses a decision to Sultan Ibragimov in Moscow, he vows to return to the ring.

In the summer of 2008, Hans Florine, along with his younger partner, 39-year-old Yuji Hirayama, scales the 2,900-foot Nose route on El Capitan, a granite formation in Yosemite National Park, in a record-breaking time of 2 hours 43 minutes and 33 seconds. (The first ascent of El Capitan, completed 50 years previously, took 47 days to complete.)

Sam Walton founds Wal-Mart.

Actress Jennifer O'Neill gets married—for the seventh time.

O. Henry publishes his most famous short story of all time, a Christmas tale titled "The Gift of the Magi."

AGE 45

George Foreman knocks out Michael Moorer to become the oldest heavyweight boxing champion in the sport's history.

Philadelphia Athletics pitcher Jack Quinn starts a World Series game, going five innings against the Chicago Cubs. The Athletics win the game 10-8.

Susan Sarandon earns the first of her three Academy Award Best Actress nominations—and gives birth to her third child.

Henry Ford introduces an automobile he dubs the Model T.

South African surgeon Christiaan Barnard completes the first successful human heart transplant.

"Thinking is the hardest work there is, which is why so few engage in it."

— HENRY FORD

Gene Rodenberry unveils a TV series he calls *Star Trek*.

Leonardo da Vinci finishes his painting *The Lord's Supper*.

Walter Cronkite assumes the role of anchor of *The CBS Evening News*.

Eccentric billionaire Howard Hughes goes into a self-imposed seclusion, where he will remain for the rest of his life.

Pastor Jerry Falwell founds a movement he calls The Moral Majority.

AGE 46

Golfer Marty Joyce becomes the first man to qualify for the finals of the Remax North American Long-Driving Championship in both the right- and left-handed categories. The teaching pro from Hillside, Illinois, drives the ball 285 yards as a lefty and 358 yards right-handed.

Experimenting with a kite during a thunderstorm, Ben Franklin discovers the presence of electricity in lightning.

"If we did not sometimes taste of adversity, prosperity would not be so welcome."

– ANNE BRADSTREET

Volleyball legend Karch Kiraly plays his final matches before finally retiring.

Charles Darrow invents a board game called Monopoly.

Michelle Triola sues her ex-lover, actor Lee Marvin, for "palimony" remuneration, creating a new legal precedent.

Jack Nicklaus shoots a final-round 65—including a stunning 30 on the back 9 holes—to become the surprise winner of The Masters tournament.

Playwright Samuel Beckett writes his masterwork, *Waiting for Godot*.

George Foreman defends his heavyweight boxing crown with a 12-round decision over Axel Schulz.

New York Giants punter Sean Landeta retires after a 25-year professional career, which includes duty in both the USFL and the NFL. He is the last alum of the long-defunct USFL still playing in the NFL.

Terminally ill computer science professor Randy Pausch delivers his famous "Last Lecture," which becomes an Internet sensation and, later, the basis of a best-selling book.

AGE 47

Evo Morales, president of Bolivia, plays 41 minutes in his debut for second-division soccer team Litoral.

Scottish bacteriologist Alexander Fleming discovers an antibiotic called penicillin.

Richard Petty wins his 200th (and final) race, Daytona's Firecracker 400, in front of 80,000 fans, including then-President Ronald Reagan.

Bill Cosby debuts as Heathcliff Huxtable in the instant-classic TV series *The Cosby Show*.

Marlon Brando stars as Don Vito Corleone in the film adaptation of Mario Puzo's novel *The Godfather*.

Physician and former collegiate runner Tom White, whose left leg was severely damaged by a drunk driver 27 years previously, undergoes elective below-the-knee amputation so that he can be fitted with a prosthetic limb and return to running.

Kate Douglas Wiggin completes her novel *Rebecca of Sunnybrook Farm*.

Darren Taylor, who performs under the name Professor Splash, plunges 35 feet 4 inches into a foot-deep pool of water to break his own Guinness world record for the highest shallow dive.

Belgian physicist Auguste Piccard becomes the first person to reach the stratosphere, and he does it via a hot-air balloon.

Joan Collins makes her debut in the prime-time soap opera *Dynasty*.

Al Unser wins his record-tying fourth Indy 500.

AGE 48

Even though he holds the points lead in auto racing's Nextel Cup, Mark Martin takes a break four races into the season to fulfill a promise to spend time with his family.

French psychologist Alfred Binet develops the first tests to measure intelligence.

Julius Boros becomes the oldest golfer to win a Major when he wins the PGA Championship by one stroke over Arnold Palmer and Bob Charles.

Kate Chopin completes her controversial novel *The Awakening*.

Mark Twain publishes *The Adventures of Huckleberry Finn*.

Producer Norman Lear unveils the groundbreaking—and controversial—TV series *All in the Family*, starring Carroll O'Connor as the bigoted Archie Bunker.

Mary Cassatt paints *The Bath*.

AGE 49

Pauline Kael begins her tour of duty as film critic for *The New Yorker*.

Chef Julia Child writes *Mastering the Art of French Cooking*.

Bram Stoker completes a novel he titles *Dracula*.

Madonna leaves her label (Warner) and signs a multiplatform deal, worth $120 million, with Live Nation.

Jeanette Roberts, a 35-handicapper, cards an amazing three aces in five rounds at the Granite Bay Golf Club. A mathematician projects that, on the average, a golfer would have to hit a tee shot on a par-3 hole every minute of every hour of every day for 5,700 years to equal Roberts's feat.

Davy Crockett dies in battle defending The Alamo.

Geraldine Ferraro runs as the 1984 Democratic vice presidential candidate (with Walter Mondale), becoming the first woman to run for the office on a major-party ticket.

Raymond Floyd wins the 1992 Doral Open golf tournament.

Jeff Foxworthy becomes one of the most watched personalities on television, hosting the game show *Are You Smarter than a 5th Grader*?

Holly Hunter tackles one of the sexiest roles in television history, playing Grace Hannadarko on the Emmy-winning *Saving Grace*.

Showing shades of his former self, John McEnroe is ejected from an opening round tennis match at the Hall of Fame Champions Cup tournament for cursing, arguing with the chair umpire, and making an obscene gesture at fans.

"The mind is at its best
about the age of 49."

— Aristotle

St. Francis College's Irma Garcia becomes the first Hispanic athletic director at a Division 1 school. (She had previously played and coached at the college.)

Susan Sarandon wins the Best Actress Oscar for her role in *Dead Man Walking*.

Just short of her fiftieth birthday, Martina Navratilova adds one more tennis championship to her long list, in the doubles competition at the U.S. Open.

AGE 50

Beverly Sills becomes director of the New York City Opera.

With a Tony Award and an Oscar already on his mantel, Sidney Sheldon turns to writing novels. His books will end up selling more than 300 million copies in 51 languages.

Race car driver Bobby Allison wins the Daytona 500—holding off a charge from his son Davey.

Charles Darwin publishes his pioneering work, *On the Origin of Species*.

Jamie Lee Curtis celebrates her fiftieth birthday by posing topless for *AARP The Magazine*. "I feel way better now than I did when I was 20," she says.

Henrik Ibsen writes his classic play *A Doll's House*.

British physician William Harvey discovers the workings of the human circulatory system.

After coming out of basketball retirement to sign a seven-day contract, Nancy Lieberman dishes out two assists in nine minutes in a WNBA game between the Detroit Shock and the Houston Comets. The experience makes Lieberman the oldest player to take the floor in WNBA history.

AGE 51

Sandra Day O'Connor becomes the first woman justice to serve on the U.S. Supreme Court.

Italian doctor Sanctorius invents the thermometer.

Seemingly ageless hockey player Gordie Howe scores his 800th NHL goal.

"I didn't invent the hamburger. I just took it more seriously than anyone else."

– Ray Kroc

Marshall McLuhan pens his famous phrase, "The medium is the message."

AGE 52

Johannes Brahms completes his fourth (and final) symphony.

Harry Gant wins the Champion 400 at the Michigan International Speedway, becoming NASCAR's oldest winner.

Sam Snead wins the Greater Greensboro Open.

Ayn Rand completes her massive novel *Atlas Shrugged*.

Julius Caesar begins a love affair with the 21-year-old Cleopatra.

Tchaikovsky composes a ballet suite called *The Nutcracker*.

Leonardo da Vinci completes the *Mona Lisa*.

Ray Kroc, a milkshake machine salesman, starts a fast-food chain called McDonald's.

AGE 53

Susan Sarandon receives her star on the Hollywood Walk of Fame.

Tennis's Chris Evert and golf's Greg Norman are wed in the Bahamas. The marriage is Norman's second, Evert's third.

Ludwig van Beethoven completes his ninth (and final) symphony.

President Abraham Lincoln issues the *Emancipation Proclamation*, which leads to freeing slaves in Confederate states.

Samuel Morse sends the first telegraph message—from Washington, D.C., to Baltimore.

Margaret Thatcher is elected as Great Britain's first female Prime Minister.

Walt Disney opens a theme park he calls Disneyland in Anaheim, California.

Minnie Minoso of the Chicago White Sox swats a base hit, becoming the oldest Major Leaguer to achieve that feat.

"Whatever you are,
be a good one."

— Abraham Lincoln

Geraldine Wesolowski gives birth to a child who is actually her grandson. She was implanted with an egg from her daughter-in-law that was fertilized by her son.

Ernest Hemingway writes *The Old Man and the Sea*.

AGE 54

South African breast cancer survivor Louise Cooper completes the 135-mile Badwater ultramarathon, just five months after completing chemotherapy treatment. (Cooper has completed races of up to 300 miles.)

Henry Heimlich makes public a choking-prevention maneuver that will eventually be named after him.

Theodor Geisel, better known as Dr. Seuss, publishes *The Grinch Who Stole Christmas*.

Janet Reno takes office as the United States' first female Attorney General.

Jockey Willie Shoemaker rides 17-to-1 longshot Ferdinand to victory in the Kentucky Derby.

Sarah Bernhardt earns acclaim for her portrayal of Hamlet.

British computer programmer Keith Straw sets a personal best of 3 hours and 12 minutes at the Boston Marathon, despite racing in a homemade pink tutu and carrying a wand.

Prohibition proponent Carrie Nation begins smashing saloons with her infamous ax.

AGE 55

Lynn Tracy, a dog trainer by trade, wins the national 10-kilometer racewalking championships for her age group, complementing her age-group victories in the 5k and 10k at the U.S. Masters National Outdoor Championships.

Johannes Gutenberg, inventor of the printing press, publishes the first mass production of the Bible. Total print run: 300 copies.

Italian physicist Alessandro Volta invents the battery.

Aging tennis pro Bobby Riggs puts up a worthy battle but loses to 29-year-old Billie Jean King in the much-hyped Battle of the Sexes.

Cary Grant stars in the action-packed Alfred Hitchcock film *North by Northwest*.

Author Alex Haley publishes his epic masterwork, *Roots*.

Ts'ai Lun, a Chinese court officer (and eunuch), develops an early version of writing paper.

AGE 56

Pistol shooter Libby Callahan, a former Washington, D.C., police sergeant, competes in her fourth Olympic Games, becoming the oldest woman in any sport to make a U.S. Olympic team.

After 24 days of work, George Handel completes his *Messiah*.

Gustave Eiffel completes the design for the Paris tower that will bear his name.

Toni Morrison finishes writing *Beloved*.

Author Norman Mailer completes *The Executioner's Song*.

"The largest room in the world is the room for improvement."

— Taylor Morgan

"From the beginning,
I imagined I would have
a long work life."

— Bruce Springsteen

AGE 57

George Washington is inaugurated as the first President of the United States, receiving all 69 electoral votes. (He will stand as the only President unanimously elected.)

Annie Peck becomes the first person to reach the summit of Mount Huascaran in the Andes.

John Handegard wins the Northwest Classic to become the oldest player to win a Professional Bowling Association event.

James Joyce publishes *Finnegans Wake*.

Power lifter Odd Haugen is featured on the National Geographic Channel as America's strongest man.

Satirical writer Jonathan Swift publishes *Gulliver's Travels*.

AGE 58

Bruce Springsteen and the E Street Band are named Best Live Band of the Year for 2008 by *Rolling Stone* magazine.

After 40 years of trying, John Dane III, a father of seven, earns a berth on the U.S. Olympic team in the Star class of the sailing event.

Karol Wojtyla, who will become better known as John Paul II, becomes Pope.

Miguel de Cervantes publishes *Don Quixote*.

Frank Sinatra, retired for two years, reignites his career.

W. H. Hoover develops an electric suction sweeper that is soon dubbed a vacuum cleaner.

Bostonian Mary Baker Eddy founds the Church of Christ, Scientist.

AGE 59

Satchel Paige pitches for the Kansas City A's, becoming the oldest pitcher—and player of any kind—to play in a Major League game.

Billy Joel performs two sold-out historic concerts in New York's Shea Stadium shortly before it is demolished. The 55,000 tickets for the opening-night show sell out in 48 minutes.

Jockey Johnny Longden wins his record-breaking 6,032nd race.

John Force earns his 1000th funny-car victory at the 2008 NHRA Nationals.

Clara Barton founds the American Red Cross.

Mike Flynt, a grandfather, plays linebacker for Sul Ross State University in Texas. His feat catches the attention of NBA star LeBron James, whose athlete management company secures a two-book contract for Flynt.

Abolitionist John Brown leads a raid on the U.S. arsenal at Harpers Ferry, Virginia.

Madeleine Albright becomes the first woman Secretary of State for the United States.

AGE **60**

Thomas Jefferson buys the Louisiana Territory from the French—for about 5 cents an acre.

Dr. Hattie Alexander discovers the cure for bacterial meningitis.

"A wise person hears one word
and understands two."

— YIDDISH PROVERB

Ruth Bader Ginsburg is appointed to the U.S. Supreme Court.

Long-retired baseball pitcher Nolan Ryan is asked to throw out a ceremonial first pitch for a game in Japan. He fires an 85-mph fastball, noting that with a couple months of training, he could throw in the low 90s.

Alfred Hitchcock directs what will arguably be his most famous film, *Psycho*.

Novelist George Eliot marries her 40-year-old broker, John Walter Cross.

Groucho Marx debuts as host of the TV quiz show *You Bet Your Life*.

AGE 61

Woodrow Wilson announces his 14-point plan to end World War I.

Sharpshooter Annie Oakley nails 98 of 100 clay pigeons in an exhibition at a North Carolina gun club.

Republican Congresswoman Jeannette Rankin casts Congress's lone dissenting vote against declaring war on Japan after the Pearl Harbor bombing.

David Ben-Gurion becomes Israel's first Prime Minister.

AGE 62

Agatha Christie pens the hit play *The Mousetrap*, which debuted in 1952 and is still running today—an all-time record.

Golfer Sam Snead finishes third at the PGA championship and second at the Los Angeles Open.

Sir Alec Guiness stars as Ben Kenobi in *Star Wars*.

Louis Pasteur inoculates his first patient against rabies.

AGE 63

Eugenicist Francis Galton demonstrates that each person's fingerprints are unique. Criminals worldwide mourn.

"A journey of a thousand miles begins with a single step."

— Confucius

Larry Hoff, a retired teacher and football coach, journeys by bicycle and canoe from Washington, D.C., to Astoria, Oregon, to complete his third nonmotorized crossing of the United States. The trek takes him 132 days.

Playboy founder Hugh Hefner weds Miss January 1988, who is 37 years his junior.

Voltaire completes his famous satirical book, *Candide*.

Alfred Hitchcock directs Tippi Hedren and a feathered supporting cast in *The Birds*.

Conductor Leopold Stokowski marries a 21-year-old woman named Gloria Vanderbilt.

AGE 64

Oscar Hammerstein crafts the lyrics for the musical *The Sound of Music*.

Betty Ford, wife of President Gerald R. Ford, opens her eponymously named clinic to treat substance abuse.

Californian Weller Noble shoots a 64 at an Oakland country club, becoming the youngest golfer to shoot his age.

Louie Armstrong records his famous version of "Hello, Dolly."

Scottish mathematician John Napier unveils an invention called the logarithm.

AGE 65

U.S. Secretary of State William Henry Seward buys the 580,000 acres of Alaska from Russia—for less than 2 cents an acre.

U.S. Surgeon General C. Everett Koop issues a report branding cigarettes as the country's No. 1 cause of preventable death.

Colonel Harland Sanders begins nationwide licensing for his special fried chicken recipe, which will come to be known as Kentucky Fried Chicken.

Laura Ingalls Wilder publishes *Little House in the Big Woods*, the first volume in her eight-part series called *Little House on the Prairie*.

Attorney William Jennings Bryant (also a three-time U.S. presidential candidate) argues the state's case in the famous Scopes Monkey Trial.

Winston Churchill takes office as Britain's Prime Minister.

Anthropologist-archaeologist Mary Leakey discovers fossilized footprints dating back 3.5 million years in Tanzania.

AGE 66

Michelangelo completes his *Last Judgment* fresco in the Sistine Chapel.

Spencer Tracy stars in *Guess Who's Coming to Dinner?*

Maggie Kuhn founds the Gray Panthers.

Adriana Iliescu of Romania gives birth to a daughter, Eliza Maria.

Michelangelo completed two
of his best-known works,
the *Pietà* and the *David*,
before he turned thirty.

"The older I get,
the better I used to be."

– Lee Trevino

AGE 67

Japanese equestrian Hiroshi Hoketsu, a dressage rider, competes at the 2008 Olympic Games, 44 years after his first Olympic competition.

Engineer Joseph Baermann Strauss celebrates as his masterwork, the Golden Gate Bridge, is opened to traffic.

Louise Boyd becomes the first woman to fly over the North Pole.

George Bernard Shaw completes his play *Saint Joan*.

John Jennings finishes third in the forty-seventh Windmill Class Association national sailing championship—47 years after he won the inaugural edition of the race.

Gynecologist John Rock begins testing a birth control pill.

AGE 68

Australian Clifford Batt swims 34-plus miles across the English Channel.

Lillian Carter, mother of President Jimmy Carter, joins the Peace Corps and works for two years as a nurse in India.

Author Henry Miller finally sees the U.S. publication of his controversial novel, *Tropic of Cancer*, which the country had banned for 27 years.

Writer Victor Hugo returns home to France after 19 years in political exile. "Dream no small dream." — *Victor Hugo*

AGE 69

Mother Teresa wins the Nobel Peace Prize.

Francis Chichester completes a solo sail across the Atlantic Ocean—4,000 miles in 22 days.

Mary Kaplan realizes her goal of running a marathon in every U.S. state—and finishing first in her age group in each race.

Laurence Olivier wins acclaim for his portrayal of the sadistic Christian Szell in the film *Marathon Man*, opposite Dustin Hoffman. The acclaimed actor earns a Golden Globe Award and an Oscar nomination.

"Love is a fruit in season
at all times, and within
reach of every hand."

— MOTHER TERESA

"'Tis not knowing much,
but what is useful,
that makes a wise person."

– Thomas Fuller, M.D.

Composer Richard Wagner completes his opera *Parsifal*.

After 22 years of work, Noah Webster publishes the land-mark *An American Dictionary of the English Language*.

Just 16 days short of his seventieth birthday, Ronald Reagan becomes the oldest U.S. President to take office.

Brigham Young fathers his fifty-sixth (and final) child.

AGE 70

Philosopher Socrates is condemned to death. His crime? Allegedly poisoning the minds of Athenian youth.

Yuichiro Miura becomes the oldest person to scale Mt. Everest.

Ramon Blanco, a former violin maker, climbs all Seven Summits, becoming the oldest person ever to do so.

Retired airline pilot George Brunstad becomes the oldest person to swim the English Channel, no doubt impressing his nephew Matt Damon.

Dr. William Mayo founds a medical clinic which will bear his name.

Author E. B. White completes the children's classic *The Trumpet of the Swan*.

Elizabeth Gurley Flynn becomes the first woman head of the U.S. Communist Party.

Writer Somerset Maugham completes *The Razor's Edge*.

AGE 71

Fashion icon Coco Chanel debuts the Chanel suit.

After 27 years in a South African prison, Nelson Mandela gains his freedom.

Joe Sweeney makes the varsity tennis team at Massachusetts's Salem State College.

John Houseman wins the Best Supporting Actor Oscar for his role as a law professor in *The Paper Chase*.

Philosopher Saint Augustine completes his epic *The City of God*.

"A woman has the age
she deserves."

– COCO CHANEL

AGE 72

At the 1920 Olympics, Swedish marksman Oscar Swahn captures the silver medal in the running deer double-shot team event, making him the oldest person to win a medal in modern Olympic history.

Karl Wallenda, of the famous Flying Wallendas, walks a high wire between the Eden Rock and Fontainebleau hotels in Miami.

Suzan Toft aces the 116-yard par 3 at England's Trentham golf course. A TV crew hears the news and asks her to repeat the feat. She grabs her 5-wood and sinks her tee shot again.

Michelangelo designs the dome for St. Peter's Basilica in Rome.

Sophocles completes the renowned play *Oedipus Rex*.

Sculptor Daniel Chester French finishes the marble figure of Abraham Lincoln, which adorns the Lincoln Memorial.

German novelist Thomas Mann completes his epic novel *Doktor Faustus*.

After 12 years, Peter Mark Roget finishes compilation of the famed Thesaurus which bears his name.

AGE 73

The amazing Walt Stack completes the grueling Ironman Triathlon in 26 hours and 20 minutes.

Author and Oscar winner Shirley MacLaine publishes her eleventh book, *Sage-ing While Age-ing*.

Ronald Reagan is reelected President of the United States.

Albert Einstein is offered the presidency of Israel. He politely declines.

Lee Strasberg, better known as an acting teacher, puts his knowledge to work in front of the camera with a major role in the Academy Award-winning *The Godfather, Part 2*.

AGE 74

Artist Claude Monet begins painting his panels of water lilies.

Ethel Andrus founds the American Association of Retired Persons (AARP).

"Arriving at one goal is the starting point to another."

– JOHN DEWEY

After 53 years in the football coaching profession—at the high school, college, and professional levels—Mouse Davis returns to the state of Oregon (where his career began) to serve as offensive coordinator for Portland State University.

AGE 75

Cecil B. DeMille directs Charlton Heston and an all-star cast in *The Ten Commandments*. (This is DeMille's second directorial exploration of this story; the first was done more than 30 years previously.)

In an "Old-Timer's" baseball game in Washington, D.C.'s RFK Stadium, Luke Appling hits a home run off of Hall of Fame pitcher Warren Spahn.

Director Akira Kurosawa finishes his epic motion picture *Ran*, his interpretation of *King Lear*.

Piano virtuoso Claudio Arrau stays busy in his seventy-fifth year, performing a total of 110 concerts.

AGE 76

Clara Barton, founder of the American Red Cross, eschews age as she rides mule wagons and works as a battlefield nurse during the Spanish-American War.

Writer Marguerite Yourcenar becomes the first woman elected to the prestigious l'Académie française in its (then) 345-year history.

Henry Fonda stars (with daughter Jane) in *On Golden Pond*, a film that will win him an Oscar—after 41 years in the business.

Thomas Jefferson begins designing buildings and developing curricula for the University of Virginia.

Sculptor Auguste Rodin marries his longtime companion Rose Beuret, whom he met when they were 23 and 20, respectively.

"One isn't necessarily born with courage, but one is born with potential."

— MAYA ANGELOU

AGE 77

Mahatma Gandhi goes on a fast in an attempt to quell religion-sparked violence in India.

Astronaut (and Senator) John Glenn returns to space on the Space Shuttle Discovery mission.

Classical guitarist Andres Segovia celebrates the birth of his son Carlos.

AGE 78

Eleanor of Aquitaine leads an army to thwart a rebellion by her grandson, Arthur, against her son, John, the King of England.

Dale Davis, who is legally blind, rolls a perfect 300 in a bowling league playoff game. The Iowa bowler has no vision in his left eye and only very blurry vision from the corner of his right eye—just enough to allow him to line up a shot in a bowling lane.

The reclusive artist Georgia O'Keeffe paints *Sky Above Clouds IV*.

H.G. Wells, who once dropped out of school at age 14, earns a doctorate degree from London University.

The ever prolific Euripides finishes another play, *Bacchae*, which some critics will call his masterwork.

Grandma Moses begins her career as a serious painter.

AGE 79

Ben Franklin invents bifocal eyeglasses.

After 35 years of work, architect Christopher Wren completes St. Paul's Cathedral in London.

Marc Chagall unveils his murals at the Metropolitan Opera House in New York City.

Giuseppe Verdi composes the opera *Falstaff*.

Though officially retired from performing, famed contralto Marian Anderson thrills the music world when she returns to the stage to perform with the Philadelphia Orchestra.

AGE **80**

Nelson Mandela celebrates his eightieth birthday by marrying for the third time; his wife is Graça Machel, an activist and widow of Mozambique's founding president.

Jessica Tandy wins her first Oscar, earning the Best Actress nod for her role in *Driving Miss Daisy*.

George Burns's work in *The Sunshine Boys* earns him his first Oscar (for Best Supporting Actor).

Pope Gregory XIII develops the Gregorian calendar.

Andy Williams, whose concerts regularly sell out at Branson's Moon River Theater, signs a book deal to write his memoirs.

Robert Penn Warren is named America's first poet laureate.

Legendary sportscaster Vin Scully celebrates half a century in the broadcast booth calling games for the Los Angeles Dodgers. (Prior to moving to L.A., Scully spent almost ten years broadcasting for the Brooklyn Dodgers.)

"In love, as in other matters,
the young are just beginners."

— Isaac Bashevis Singer

AGE 81

Dancer/actor Fred Astaire marries 37-year-old jockey Robyn Smith.

Amos Alonzo Stagg is named college football's Coach of the Year. (He will eventually have a college bowl game named in his honor.)

The legendary Joe Paterno begins his forty-third year as head football coach for Penn State.

Barbara McClintock's groundbreaking work in genetics earns her the Nobel Prize for Physiology or Medicine.

Florida bowler Jerry Wehman rolls a perfect 300 game.

The legendary John Huston directs the film *The Dead*, his fortieth.

AGE 82

Ted Corbitt, known as the Father of American Distance Running, covers 303 miles in a six-day race.

Thelma Pitt-Turner completes the Hastings Marathon, covering the 26.2-mile course in 7 hours and 58 minutes.

Henri Matisse crafts *The Swimming Pool*, using his famed "cutout" art method.

Johann Wolfgang von Goethe completes *Faust*.

Actress Cloris Leachman joins the cast for the TV program *Dancing With the Stars*.

James Cagney costars in the movie *Ragtime*.

Writer George Bernard Shaw wins the Best Screenplay Academy Award for *Pygmalion*, making him the only person to win both a Nobel Prize and an Oscar.

AGE 83

Winston Churchill publishes the last installment of his four-volume *A History of the English-Speaking Peoples*.

Author/child psychologist Benjamin Spock is arrested for protesting the Vietnam War.

Igor Stravinsky composes the *Requiem Canticles*.

Sigmund Freud pens *Moses and Monotheism*.

Samuel Smith, a veteran of the War of 1812, leads the Maryland state militia to quell riots in Baltimore. He is later elected mayor of the city.

AGE 84

Actress Lydia Yeamans Titus makes her screen debut in the Rudolph Valentino film *All Night*.

Pablo Casals earns rave reviews for his cello recital at the Kennedy White House.

Naval commander Andrea Doria sails to battle against the Barbary pirates.

AGE 85

Celestine III is elected Pope.

After a 66-year wait, University of Hawaii quarterback Mun Kim Wong finally receives his varsity letter at a charity banquet honoring Hawaii's great quarterbacks. Wong quarter-backed the 1941 Rainbow Warriors, leading them to an 8-1 record before their season was cut short by the attack on Pearl Harbor. (On December 7, 1941, Wong enlisted with the Hawaii Territorial Guard, where he spent five years defending the Islands.)

Bertrand Russell unveils the international peace symbol.

Marvel Comics superhero creator Stan Lee's creates an anime graphic novel, develops a line of comics for Virgin mogul Richard Branson, and produces an animated series based loosely on the lives of Hugh Hefner and Ringo Starr. Lee also appears in a cameo role in the feature-film version of *Iron Man*.

Linus Pauling publishes his book *How to Live Longer and Feel Better*. (Proving he is well-qualified to author such a title, Pauling will live to be 93.)

AGE 86

Robert Frost recites his poem "The Gift Outright" at John F. Kennedy's Presidential inauguration.

"Winter is on my head,
but eternal spring
is in my heart."

– Victor Hugo

Thomas Hobbes completes his translation of Homer's *Odyssey*.

AGE 87

Jeanette Rankin, Congress's first female member—
and only congressperson to vote against declaring war on
Japan—leads an anti-Vietnam War protest on Capitol Hill.

Mary Baker Eddy launches *The Christian Science Monitor*.

Veteran actor Sir John Gielgud appears in the movie
Prospero's Books.

Pathologist Francis Peyton Rous wins the Nobel Prize for
Chemistry for his work in discovering viruses that cause cancer.

AGE 88

Michelangelo completes his sculpture *Rondandini Pieta*,
depicting an aged man holding Christ.

Helen Hooven Santmyer sees her novel . . . *And Ladies of
the Club* hit the best-seller lists.

Austrian physicist Lise Meitner wins the Enrico Fermi Prize for her work in the field of nuclear fission.

Florida Democrat Claude Pepper wins election to the U.S. House of Representatives. (Pepper, a House member for 26 years, will die in office during his thirteenth term.)

AGE 89

Architect Frank Lloyd Wright completes the Guggenheim Museum.

Though she had to stop painting at age 85 due to failing eyesight, Georgia O'Keeffe authors a book about her artistry.

Jazz pianist Eubie Blake launches a publishing/recording company.

Classical pianist Arthur Rubinstein performs his famous concert at New York's Carnegie Hall.

Edmond Hoyle (of According to Hoyle fame), having already established himself as the foremost authority on card games, writes an authoritative book on chess.

Author James Michener continues his prolific career with the publication of *This Noble Land*.

AGE 90

Sophocles writes the epic drama *Oedipus at Colonus*.

Nelson Mandela is featured on the cover of *Time* magazine in an issue that highlights his "eight secrets of leadership."

Swimmer Walt Pfeiffer sets six World Masters records at a meet in Long Beach. In the process, he becomes the first nonagenarian to complete the 400-meter individual medley.

Key Old Testament figure Sarah gives birth to her only child, Isaac.

Actress Fay Wray is honored at the seventy-eighth Academy Awards, as host Billy Crystal presents a tribute to her long film legacy.

Arthur C. Clarke completes his final novel, *The Last Theorem*. (He will review the final version of the manuscript just days before his death.)

"One good head is better than a hundred strong hands."

— Thomas Fuller, M.D.

AGE 91

Hulda Crooks summits Mount Whitney, the continental United States' highest peak.

Actor/philanthropist Kirk Douglas dedicates his 401st Los Angeles-area playground. Douglas and his wife, Anne, began rebuilding playgrounds when he was 80, and he punctuates each playground completion by zipping down the slide.

Californian Maude Tull obtains a driver's license for the first time.

Actor Ernest Borgnine celebrates the publication of his long-awaited memoir, titled *Ernie*.

AGE 92

George Burns plays a younger character (81) in the movie *18 Again* and also records a hit single by the same name.

P. G. Wodehouse publishes another book in the *Jeeves* series, *Aunts Aren't Gentlemen*.

George Bernard Shaw writes the play *Shakes Versus Shav*.

AGE 93

Artist Marc Chagall completes two paintings, *Scene de Cirque* and *The Great Parade*. (The latter painting is four years in the making.)

Republican Senator Strom Thurmond (South Carolina) is reelected for his eighth term.

Seventy-two years after starring in the groundbreaking film *The Birth of a Nation*, Lillian Gish stars in *The Whales of August*.

AGE 94

Conductor Leopold Stokowski signs a six-year recording contract.

AGE 95

Union organizer Mother Jones writes her autobiography.

Alistair Cooke delivers his final broadcast of the BBC radio series *Letter From America* before retiring. Cooke hosted the show for 58 years, making it the longest-running series in history.

AGE 96

Pablo Casals conducts the Israel Festival Youth Orchestra as it performs a Mozart symphony.

AGE 97

Wisconsin resident Simon Stern divorces his wife, Ida, six years his junior.

AGE 98

In Athens, Greece, Dimitrion Yordanidis runs a marathon in 7 hours and 33 minutes.

AGE 99

Golfer Otto Bucher cards a hole in one on the 130-yard twelfth hole at Spain's La Manga golf course.

AGE 100 (AND BEYOND)

British stage actress Gwen Ffrangcon-Davies, age 100, appears in the Sherlock Holmes movie *The Master Blackmailer*.

Ichijirou Araya, age 100, climbs Mount Fuji.

Australian Minnie Munro, age 102, marries a younger man, 83-year-old Dudley Reid, in New South Wales.

Sam Dana, the oldest living former National Football League player, celebrates 104 years on the planet some 79 years after playing his last game. He says of football, "I love this game. I loved it then, and I love it now. I wish I could still play."

After making her stage debut in 1911, Gwen Ffrangcon-Davies enjoys an 80-year career.

Educator/research scientist Ray Crist, age 104, finally retires after an almost 80-year career that began at Columbia University.

New Hampshire 111-year-old Virginia Muise, the oldest person in New England, celebrates the Boston Red Sox World Series victory. Virginia, who was born before Babe Ruth, faithfully kept a Red Sox cap on her nightstand during her team's long World Series drought.

Frenchwoman Jeanne Louise Calment celebrates her 122nd birthday. She attributes her longevity, in part, to her faithful bike riding, a practice she followed until age 100.

*

"The great pleasure in life
is doing what people say
you cannot do."

IF YOU'VE ENJOYED THIS BOOK,
WE WOULD LOVE TO HEAR FROM YOU.
WRITE TO US AT:

Hallmark Book Feedback
P.O. Box 419034
Mail Drop 215
Kansas City, MO 64141

booknotes@hallmark.com

✳

*And if you know of significant age-related feats
you'd like to see in a future edition of this book,
we'd love to hear about those, too.*